LIVING IN THE NOW

A GUIDE TO LIVING A MORE FULFILLED LIFE

D1738670

Living in the NOW
A Guide to Living a More Fulfilled Life

First Printing

Printed in the United States of America

Published by:
Darcon Publishing
5590 Cedar Creek Road
Glenville, West Virginia 26351

ISBN 978-0-9831939-0-6

Library of Congress Control Number:
2010942368

1. Self-help. 2. Psychology. 3. Relationships.
4. How-to. I. Title.

To My Wife, Ann

And Dayton,

Who have fulfilled my life beyond measure.

Table of Contents

Introduction

Another "self-help" book: Just what the world needs, right? Well, possibly. Many times books classified as "self-help" are filled with hokum, or are at the very least littered with it throughout. Or, perhaps they take a "cookie cutter" approach to addressing issues. This book, hopefully, does none of the above.

What I have tried to present are thoughts related to some of the more common issues I address in therapy, on almost a weekly basis. My hope is that by making this information available, that perhaps someone might be able to find inspiration in my words, and that I in some way might be able to help the reader.

It is my sincere hope you find something in these pages which you can apply to your life. By no means is this volume a comprehensive guide to relationships or life. Life does not come with an instruction manual. Take what you need from what you read. Use what you can. Ignore what does not apply to you.

This book has no chapters, and is intended to be read a section at a time. Whether you read a few sections at bed time, or while "taking care of business" on the porcelain throne, it is intended to not be a "chore" to read.

Some points in the book overlap. This is because life itself "overlaps." Areas from one area of our life affect others. For example, you might find that ways to celebrate your successes could also double as a romantic interlude for you and your partner. As another example, simple ways to enjoy your life might also coincide with finding ways to relax prior to going to bed. No section in this book exists in isolation, just as the various parts of your life do not.

So where to begin? To quote Glinda, The Good Witch of the South, "It's always best to start at the beginning!" And so we shall.

Why Live in the NOW?

We live in a culture that teaches us to always be thinking ahead, and plan for tomorrow. We work so we can retire. We plan so that we can have a time, be it an undefined time, that we can find enjoyment, have an adventure, see the world, etc. What about today?

I have known far too many people in my life who have planned for the future, only to have life snatched away from them. My father retired early, and within a year of his retirement was diagnosed with a debilitating brain tumor. He lived for seven years, and the happiness he planned was never realized.

Realize the reality of today. Live for the moment. Plan for the future, but live in the NOW. Take time to, "stop and smell the roses," literally. Enjoy the present. Know that if you do, you will have a more fulfilled life.

What is Important?

There is a time management technique introduced by Steven Covey that asks you to determine what is important versus what is urgent. This is an excellent technique to put tasks into perspective, and much has been written with respect to prioritizing issues in your life.

The technique we are referring to involves deciding what is *urgent*, what is *important*. How? By deciding where in an "Importance Matrix" it needs to be placed. Here is an example of an "Importance Matrix."

	Important	Not Important
Urgent		
Not Urgent		

Urgent tasks are deadline based. This is usually independent of you and is often driven by others. The sooner the task needs completion the more urgent it is. This has no relation to importance.

The importance of a job drives how much 'time' you want to spend on it. Notice that this is independent of 'urgency' and is what you *want* to do not the amount of time you actually spend on it. For any task the quality of your output will often relate to the time you spend on it.

The question then becomes, how do you personally define that which is important to you? This is a decision that you must make on your own. Ask yourself: What needs to be done? What should be done, but can wait? Make sure you factor in relationships into your "Importance Matrix" as well. The placement of items is up to you, and should be based on your personal needs and wants.

Who (Or What) Rules Your Time?

One thing that people tend to forget is that there are a great number of day to day activities that consume our NOW. A ringing telephone is a prime example. When the telephone rings, most people answer it. Where is it written that just because a telephone rings that it must be answered? A telephone is there for our convenience.

> *Where is it written that just because a telephone rings that it must be answered?*

If you are taking a moment for yourself and the telephone rings, learn to ignore it. The world will not stop, time will not cease, and you will become more attuned to the NOW in which you are reveling.

In a similar vein, my cousin had a friend who said, "Just because someone wants to talk to me, does not mean I necessarily want to talk to them." There is much wisdom in this statement.

You decide who consumes your time. In the end, you rule your time. Enjoy the power.

Slow Down

Over the course of the last few years I have attended a number of workshops on primitive skills. One of the exercises utilized by the workshop leaders is for about 30 minutes to an hour participants are to move at about ¼ of the speed that they normally do. In addition to this, participants also make as little noise as possible.

This slowing down allows us to get in tune with what they call "Earth Time." The fascinating thing is that when you cease the exercise and begin to move at your regular pace, it almost seems wrong to do so.

Slowing down expands your awareness. Doing this exercise on occasion in your daily life helps put the hectic pace of life in perspective. By engaging in this exercise, you become more acutely aware of all the hustle and bustle around you. More importantly, you can learn to separate yourself from it.

Take a Walk and Smell the Roses

What types of things can you do to help you live in the NOW? Perhaps take a walk. A leisurely walk is a wonderful way of taking a break from the day and it gives you time to reflect on what is happening in the world and in your life.

A leisurely walk is a wonderful way of taking a break from the day....

In addition to giving you a break and focusing you on the NOW, it is also good for you physically. Walking is good exercise. Getting out for a gentle stroll is good for the body as well as the soul. Focus on slowing down when you walk, and take time for yourself.

Breathe. Live. Enjoy.

Don't be FOOLED by the **calendar**. There are only as many **days** in the **year** as you make use of.

~Charles Richards

As you grow **older**, you'll find the ONLY things you **regret** are the things you DIDN'T do.

~Zachary Scott

Define Your Goals

Create a list of your goals. Indeed, it sounds hokey, but the truth is that it is a highly effective way of accomplishing what you want to accomplish. Each spring, my wife and I sit down and develop a list of tasks we want to accomplish over the course of the summer. Some folks might call this a "honey-do list," but when developed together, it becomes a "we-do list."

This list goes in a prominent place (in our case on the refrigerator) so that we can see it daily. As we accomplish a task, either individually or jointly, we mark it from the list. It is truly amazing how much we accomplish over the course of the next few months, until the weather changes.

Make your list. When you are looking for something to do, all you need to do is check the list. Any type of task can go on the list, be it simple or involved. Make your list, and watch as your accomplishments grow.

Empty Your Mind

Sometimes your mind is full of chatter. It is during these times that we often find it is difficult to slow down and live in the NOW. This can happen especially as you lie down at night to sleep.

Your mind becomes overwhelmed with thoughts of worry or anxiety, or we ruminate over what we did during the course of the day. We concentrate on what we did today, and what we can work on tomorrow.

We fail to focus on the NOW as we try to go to sleep. Sleep is a time when we need to rest and recharge our batteries. How can we make the "noise" in our minds stop, so that we can be more rested? Try these techniques. Keep in mind that not every technique works for everyone. You need to choose techniques that work for you.

The Techniques

1. Read a good book. Reading before you go to bed is an excellent way to expand your knowledge base as well as calm you down for a good night's sleep.

2. Make sure that the room is comfortable for you. Your bedroom should be your sanctuary. Do everything in your power to ensure that your bedroom is only used for sleeping, and not used as an office or exercise room, or anything else. This is the place where you sleep.

3. Practice deep breathing and progressive relaxation. Take a deep breath and tighten each muscle in your body, starting with those in your feet. Inhale…tighten the muscles…slowly exhale and relax as you do. Progressively move up your body. End with the muscles in your face. As you continue to relax you will become more prepared to sleep.

4. Imagine that you are sinking deeply into your mattress. Imagine the weight of the day pulling you into a realm of comfortableness that exceeds your wildest dreams. Melt into your mattress.

5. Do a mindless mental task. What you want is to passively relax. Sing a song in your mind, think of mentally telling yourself a story from your childhood, such as "The Three Little Pigs." It's o.k. to tell yourself a bedtime story.

6. Explore someplace in your mind. Relive exploring someplace you have already been, or perhaps you could "visit" someplace in your mind that you have never been previously.

7. As you go to bed, focus on the fact that you are going to go to sleep easily, and that you are going to have a good night's sleep. Prep yourself for success.

8. Ask your doctor about a sleep aid. There is no shame in utilizing a tool of modern science to help

you go to sleep, especially if doing so will benefit you.

Don't Let "Bad Thoughts" Control You

There are times when our minds are just full and running over with thoughts. Good thoughts, bad thoughts, anxious thoughts, etc. We are sometimes the victim of our thoughts. We have those times when we "bad mouth" ourselves.

They only have the power over you that you give to them.

It is times like these that we just need to "thank" our mind for its thoughts and let them go. Don't try to judge your thoughts as good or bad. Simply acknowledge them, and let them go. Accept them for what they are; thoughts…and nothing more. They only have the power over you that you give to them.

Attitude is a LITTLE thịng that *makes* a **big** difference.

~Winston Churchill

Every thought is *a* SEED. If

you plant CRAB apples,

DON'T **count** on

HARVESTING *Golden*

Delicious.

~Bill Meyer

Some DAYS **there** won't be A song in your heart. *Sing* **anyway.**

~Emory Austin

Does It Really Make a Difference?

Why is it that we let the little things in life distract us from living in the NOW? I have talked with so many people who allow themselves to get so upset by the little things in life.

For example, some people get so upset because they don't get their bed made every day. Is not making up your bed going to cause the world to cease to rotate? No. Does it make you a bad person because you did not make your bed? No. It makes you a person who did not make their bed. Bad people fall into a completely different category.

The question you have to ask yourself is this: "Will doing/not doing _____ make a difference a week from now? A month from now? A year from now?" If the answer is "Yes," then it warrants some thought. If not, then why let it consume you? Live in the NOW and let the little things go.

Enjoy Your Meals

One of my favorite things to do in life is to eat! Each meal is a symphony of flavors playing out on my pallet. To some, eating is simply a way to gain energy to live. To others (like me!) eating becomes something that I look forward to experiencing.

Savor each bite. Use all your senses to enjoy your meal. Chew your

> *Use all your senses to enjoy your meal.*

food slowly to savor each and every bite. Notice the texture of the food in your mouth, as well as the flavor.

Doing all of this does more than just allow you to enjoy the meal. It gives your body time to register the feeling of fullness of the stomach and reduces the tendency to overeat. So, if you are like me, and you like to eat, at least make eating work in your favor!

What Triggers Your Emotions?

Stay in tune with your emotions. This can be more difficult for some people than others, especially if you have a predisposition toward depression or anxiety. Still, sometimes if we are angry perhaps it is really a different emotion manifesting as anger. Perhaps we are afraid, or anxious, or any number of emotions.

Try to learn to gauge your emotional barometer. Generally we can feel a mood creeping up on us. Try to identify "triggers" which allow you to recognize a mood change. Triggers can be anything. Once you learn to recognize what your personal triggers are, you can learn to deal with them. How?

1. Focus on returning to the here and NOW.
2. Do what you can to rectify the situation.
3. Find the silver lining in the cloud.
4. See each trigger that you identify as a positive step toward personal growth.

Ask yourself periodically, "How am I feeling right NOW." Be honest with yourself. Are you tired? Are you irritable? Then, try to figure out a connection. To what event can you trace your feelings? This is your "trigger." Learn what your "triggers" are, and you will learn to be more in charge of your feelings.

A Simple "Meditation" Technique

1. Sit quietly in a comfortable chair. Close your eyes. Begin to focus on your breath and your breathing. Don't try to change your breathing, just simply become aware and acknowledge it. What types of things do you notice?

2. Focus on your body. Notice the pressure of the chair as it supports you. Feel the floor beneath your feet. What can you sense? What sensations do you notice?

3. Allow yourself to experience whatever feelings come into your mind. If stray thoughts come into

your mind, thank your mind for its thoughts and let them go. Focus on living in the NOW.

4. Begin by doing this for about 5 minutes a day. Try to work yourself up to 20-30 minutes per session, once per day. Take it slowly. Work your way to 30 minutes over the course of a month or two. RELAX and ENJOY!

Relationships

To quote the great philosopher Jimmy Buffett, "Relationships...we've all got 'em......now what do we do with 'em." Our personal relationships are the most important things in our lives, yet we spend very little time actively working on them or thinking about them. We have two options when it comes to our relationships. We can either passively let

Relationships are like a garden.

them "happen," or we can actively nurture them.

Relationships are like a garden. We need to plant seeds of kindness, water them with compassion, remove the weeds through understanding, and enjoy their bounty. In doing so, they will provide us with a lifetime of fare! Don't wait for a friend to call you, call them! You don't need to have a reason to send a card, send one!

Be Still and Listen

Ask someone how they are doing, and then just LISTEN. Don't focus on what you are going to tell them…listen to what they tell you. It is amazing how much we miss simply because our mind is focused on what *we* want to say. Friends and loved ones need to talk, to chat, or to vent. Simply listen and let them get it all out of their system.

As an exercise, try to start conversations in which you make the conversation all about the other person! A little effort goes a long way. If you do this enough, people will acknowledge you as a "good listener," and someone they can talk with about their problems…..someone who really cares.

If You Talk the Talk, Walk the Walk

What you do is as important as what you say. In therapy we look for congruency between what a person says and what a person does. If they match, then this is good. If they do not, then there is an underlying issue. We then focus on trying to answer why incongruity exists. Sometimes people are unaware of their lack of congruency.

As I was writing this, I thought of an example that helps to make the idea more clear. Try to think of a bad actor in a B movie. Notice how they say something that is angry, but they don't *really* seem angry? They are incongruent. People's incongruent behaviors can be this blatant, but sometimes they can be more subtle.

What do your actions say about you? What do your actions reveal about you to your friends? Take time to examine your deeds.

Keep Your Friends As Near As Possible

Stay in touch with your friends as much as possible. Keep an assortment of cards handy so that you can send them when the mood strikes you to do so. Use the various social networking sites on the internet to keep in touch with your friends.

Keep in mind that getting a letter or a card from a friend can brighten someone's day. I recently had a birthday, and over 100 friends on a popular social networking site I use wished me a

> *Use the various social networking sites on the internet to keep in touch with your friends.*

Happy Birthday. It really lifted my spirits and I am grateful that I have that many people in my life who took the time to let me know they were thinking about me.

Send someone a "virtual gift." Even getting an "e-card" makes us feel good. Simple acts such as these help us to nurture our relationships and let people know we care.

The MOST beautiful *discovery*
true friends make **is** THAT
they **can** *grow* separately without
growing APART.

~ Elizabeth Foley

WHO finds **a** FAITHFUL
friend, finds a treasure.

~ Jewish saying

A FAITHFUL **friend** IS
THE *medicine of* life.

~ Apocrypha

The Golden Rule, And Then Some

Remember the Golden Rule? Various cultures have similar philosophical sayings, but generally it goes something like:

> *"Do unto others as you would have them do unto you."*

How about taking it one step further?

> *"Give that which you wish to receive."*

If you want to receive kindness, give kindness to others. Give respect and understanding, and watch how you receive the same in return.

Will this happen in every case? No, and it isn't rational to expect it. You give these things freely, without expecting them in return. However, you are more likely to be treated with respect if you treat others with respect. Focus on yourself, and allow yourself to be respected and the kind of person that you know you are.

It's Worth Repeating….Be Still And Listen

You need to learn that you are only in charge of yourself. You cannot change anyone, except yourself. You must learn that you have no control over others. You cannot make others "feel" a specific way. You are responsible for your own feelings, as are they. If someone you care about has a problem, it is their problem to own, and not yours. Know that by trying to make their problem your own, you do them no good.

If a friend wants to talk to you about their problem, LISTEN. Don't offer advice; don't tell them what you would do. Simply listen. Sometimes people just need a friend to listen to them, and by telling a friend what is on their minds, they feel better. LISTEN when other people talk. Don't worry about what you have to say, or about trying to tell them something similar that happened in your life. Be still, and listen.

Advice From You

Be careful about giving advice. To quote J.R.R. Tolkien, "Advice is a dangerous gift, even from the wise to the wise, and all courses may run ill." What works for me may not work for another. It is better that a person makes their own choices rather than rely on the choices of another.

What if the advice you give them takes your friend down the wrong path?

Of course, let's use some sense in this. If you have expertise in some area or know more about something than another person i.e., how to fix a water heater or some other applicable situation, that's one thing, but matters of personal and emotional consequence are quite another. If someone asks you about a problem they are having with their water heater, then of course, it is good to give them insight. But if it involves matters of the heart or with major life decisions, then hold back.

What if the advice you give them takes your friend down the wrong path? What if it hurts them more than it helps them? Do you want this on your conscious? Be very careful before saying, "If I were you, I would....." You will never be that person, and you won't be the one living with the consequences if they take your advice.

If you do have to give advice, do so carefully. Think about what you are saying. Acknowledge the limitations of your position in giving advice and qualify what you say by adding a disclaimer.

Advice From Others

What if someone tries to give you advice? Sometimes the way they offer the advice might come across as criticism. At the very least, it can be potentially perceived as such, even when that wasn't the intent.

Keep in mind that many times they are most likely saying these things because they care about you. Keep this in mind before you respond harshly to their words.

Unconditional Positive Regard

The famous humanist Carl Rogers coined the term, "Unconditional Positive Regard." What does this mean? It means to accept others in spite of what they might say, do, believe, etc. We acknowledge their worth even though we may not

> *...suspend judgment when dealing with others.*

agree their actions. In other words, if someone exhibits a behavior we do not agree with, we must learn to separate the behavior from the person. If someone's behavior is upsetting to you and you wish to talk to the person about it, it is suggested that you use "I Statements." An example of this would be, "When you [do whatever it is that you find upsetting],

I feel [tell them how you feel]." The key then is to wait and listen to their response.

Remember, it is essential that you "attack" the behavior, and *not* the person. A person's first instinct will most likely be to become defensive. This is natural. Stay calm and focused, knowing that it is the person's behavior with which you have issue, not the person.

Fret Not

So many people spend so much time fretting over the past or worrying about the future. Interestingly, those times are all outside of our reach. We live in the NOW. We live in this moment. We can do nothing about the past, as what's done is done. The only control we have over the future is what we do NOW.

Regarding Regrets

Everyone has wishes and regrets. Everyone has something from their past that troubles them. Granted, some have had a more troublesome past than others. However, for all of us, that time is gone. We cannot go back and change things.

Regrets only hold you back, and do not allow you to move into the potential positivity of the NOW. Living in the NOW allows us to take what we have learned from our past and make a better future. At some point in time, our future will be our NOW, and it is at that time we will realize the fruits of our labors.

Remember, just because you have something you regret from your past does not mean that you cannot have a fulfilled NOW and a fulfilled future. Let your regrets go.

The Charger And The Miller

A horse, which had been used to carry his rider into battle felt himself growing old and chose to work in a mill instead. He now no longer found himself stepping out proudly to the beating of the drums, but was compelled to slave away all day grinding corn.

Bewailing his hard lot, he said one day to the miller, "Ah me! I was once a splendid war-horse, gaily caparisoned, and attended by a groom whose sole duty it was to see to my wants. How different is my present condition! I wish I had never given up the battlefield for the mill."

The miller replied with asperity, "It's no use your regretting your past. Fortune has many ups and downs: you must take them as they come."

-Aesop

Carpe Momentum, NOW!

Perhaps you have heard the saying, *"Carpe Diem"* which means, "seize the day." Instead I suggest to you, *"Carpe Momentum!"* Seize the moment! Do you want to live in the past? You cannot. Do you live in the future? You cannot. You are alive in the NOW, and can only live in the NOW. Seize the moment. Take advantage of where you are NOW.

Personal Goals

Goals are important. We spoke previously about having a "To-Do" list on the refrigerator. Here's a quick question. Do you have a list of goals? A list of goals is just as important as a "To-Do" list. It provides you with focus to accomplish the bigger things in life that you want to accomplish.

Goals are more encompassing than a "To-Do" list. Indeed, your "To-Do" list could help you work toward your goals, and in fact it should. In

Behaviorism there is a technique known as shaping, in which we slowly change and modify behaviors until we get the desired result, or as they also call it, "the method of successive approximation."

Allow your "To-Do" list to shape the little things in life to help achieve your overall goals. Want a beautifully landscaped lawn? Do it by installing one flower/shrub bed at a time. Put that one bed on your "To-Do" list, and work toward getting it completed. After it is finished, add another. Want to go to Rome on vacation? Put "Save $500 in six months in a cookie jar," on your "To-Do" list. Start sticking a little money in a cookie jar, and work toward getting $500 over the next six months. Keep doing this every 6 months until you have enough to go.

Do a little at a time. By using your things "To-Do" you can accomplish your overall goals!

Learn to say "No."

It is OK to say, "No." The world will not collapse if you elect not to do something. Saying no is not a selfish act. Indeed, it is quite the opposite. The simple act of saying no can be one of the best things you can do for your family as well as other commitments.

By saying no to various commitments, you can spend more quality time with your family, as well as being able to focus on those things that are important to you.

"But We've Always Done It That Way!"

Just because you've always done something does not mean that you have to continue to do it. As an example, suppose you are the one who has always organized the family reunion. It does not mean that you absolutely have to do it this year. Where is it written that YOU have to do it? Are you going to guilt yourself into doing it by saying, "If I don't do it, no one else will." If it is important to other people, it will get done. If it isn't it then it won't be done. It's that simple. Which then begs the question; is this your reunion, or theirs? Life will go on without a reunion. My graduating class has never had a single reunion, and we are approaching 25 years. Has the world stopped turning? No. Have people died as a result of not having this gathering? No. It's OK to not do things. Give yourself a break.

Also, saying YES all the time isn't good for you. Being overly committed can cause a great deal of personal stress, which could eventually start to wear you down physically. When this happens, it is possible that you can become seriously tired or ill. Or worse! You might get a bad case of the "Grouch-butt" (as my wife likes to call it). "Grouch-butt" afflicts almost everyone at one time or another, and can have a detrimental effect on relationships. It is best to limit your stress, thus avoiding a chronic or acute case of "Grouch-butt."

All this is fine, but how do you learn to say no? First of all, don't fabricate excuses or reasons to get out of an obligation. The truth is always the best way to deal with this type of situation. Eventually if you fabricate excuses, one will come back to haunt you. Also, when you do tell people no, try to be as positive with them as possible. Thank them for asking you to participate, compliment their efforts, congratulate them, etc., whatever is appropriate for the situation.

Here is a simple script you can follow:

They ask you to do whatever.

You say, "Oh...I'm sorry, but I can't. I appreciate you asking me though. I really think (throw in a compliment about the event or request), but I've got so many commitments now, and I'm really stretched thin. Thanks again for asking me though..."

If they persist after you have said no, think about your family or something else meaningful and reaffirm that you cannot fulfill the obligation. If they continue, then feel free to tell them that they are putting you in an awkward situation.

Know that it will not be easy to start saying no, especially if you are accustom to saying yes all the time. With practice you will get better at it, and if you are inclined to feel guilt when telling people no, it will become less and less.

Different Strokes for Different Folks

At some point you will need to realize that there is more than one way to look at things or to do things. It does not make any difference what those "things" might be, but assuredly there are multitudes of ways of approaching how to deal with them. On the surface, people might acknowledge this, but do they really accept it? Many times, the answer is no.

Just because someone has a difference of opinion, or a different way of doing something does not make their way or their perspective wrong. It is just different.

Right and wrong imply a value judgment. Shakespeare said it best, in Hamlet, Act II- Scene II: "…for there is nothing either good or bad, but thinking makes it so…" If you feel that there is a "right" way to do something, then you are implying that you know best, because your way is right.

> "…for there is nothing either good or bad, but thinking makes it so…"
> *Hamlet - Act II, Scene II*

Thus, if your way is right, any other way must be wrong. You may not think that this is the case, but this is often how these situations are perceived by others, especially when we start telling others how they should be conducting themselves or how they should be doing things.

Why does there have to be a right and wrong way to do something? Try looking at it in the sense that other people's ways of doing things are not the way you do them, but hey....if it works for them....so be it. It is, after all, their lives...not yours. You can only make yourself happy, and if dwelling on the way that "other people do things" you are focusing on something over which you have no control.

OOPS! Mistakes

Understand that mistakes happen. You are not perfect, nor is anyone else. Try to keep this in mind when you don't get exactly what you order at the drive-thru, or when something does not go as planned because of an error.

This isn't to say that if the same mistakes happen frequently that you should not address the issue, but this does not mean that you need to do so in negative way. Give people a break. Wouldn't you want one?

I have to admit, that sometimes I am a bit brusque with people, but this is the exception to my behavior, and not the rule. What about you? Are you known to be someone who reacts negatively when something goes awry? Or, are you known as someone who is understanding? How would you like to be perceived? Keep in mind that it is OK to react to a situation, but it is not OK to over-react.

Embrace Your Emotions

Do fulfilled people not experience emotions? Do they not get angry, or depressed? Goodness no! To deny your feelings is to deny your humanity.

It is OK to feel whatever you feel, and you are entitled to every emotion that you experience. The trick is to react, but not over-react. Feel angry....but not to the point it becomes detrimental. Be saddened by another person's loss, but not to the point that it impairs you. Keep things in perspective. Acknowledge the emotion, but ask yourself if you are overreacting. If you feel that you are, then it is time to gather yourself, take a step back, and examine yourself.

Do Not Ignore Your Problems......
They Won't Go Away

It is important that we face situations which we find to be difficult head-on. It is irrational to believe that it is easier to avoid issues and problems than it is to deal with them. Avoiding problems does not make them go away, and in fact stretches out the amount of time they have power over us.

The relief that you get from putting off dealing with a situation is only temporary.

The relief that you get from putting off dealing with a situation is only temporary, while dealing with an issue gets it out of your way and provides a more permanent sense of relief. Life is for living, and hiding from different aspects of it only limits your fulfillment.

When you encounter a situation that is difficult, recognize it for what it is. Look at it rationally and logically, and ACCURATELY assess how negative it is. Do not give in to "catastrophizing," i.e., allowing yourself to feel that your world is ending or your life is ruined because of the event or situation. The world will go on, and so will you.

Deal with your issues and feel the freedom doing so will bring. Don't allow them to have power over you. Don't allow them to consume your life. Understand that you and you alone can end their "reign of terror" in your life.

By giving issues power over you, you take away from your energy to live in the NOW. By dealing with your issues you can focus your energy on more productive aspects of living. Free yourself. Take back your life. Ignoring things does not make them go away. At some point, you've got to get out of bed and face the day.

We CANNOT waste **time**.
We can only *waste*
ourselves.

~George M. Adams

The **more** side roads you
stop to **explore**, the less
LIKELY that life will **pass**
you by.

~Robert Brault

Be Well...Physically and Emotionally

It is essential that you have regular check-ups by a trusted physician. In order to live a fulfilled life, keeping an eye on your physical condition is very important.

What many people do not realize is that certain physical conditions can affect your emotional and psychological wellbeing. One example of this would be hypo- or hyperthyroidism. Issues with your thyroid can cause you to feel depressed or anxious even to the point of having panic attacks. Imagine if you are feeling exceptionally depressed or anxious, and the cause can be discovered and by a simple blood test.

Physical health and mental health go hand in hand. In order to be healthy and fulfilled, we need to understand that we must look at ourselves in totality. If you do not feel well physically, it is likely that you won't feel well emotionally as well. Stay well.

Give Yourself A Pat On The Back

Celebrate your accomplishments! It is ok to acknowledge that you have done well and accomplished something. How? Well, there are multitudes of ways. Treat yourself to something, be it a meal at a restaurant that you like, a movie, an evening out with friends, etc.

Know also that treating yourself does not mean that you have to spend money. You could plan a special get together with friends, perhaps a pot-luck party. An evening with friends, having fun, laughing, and enjoying each other's company is an excellent way to celebrate. Refer to page 135 in the Appendix for a list of suggestions on low-cost to no-cost ways to celebrate and reward yourself.

One word of caution: You do need to be careful about how you treat yourself. Buying something for yourself may not be the best idea in all cases. It may stretch you financially, put you behind for the next month (in terms of having money to pay bills), and frankly, physical possessions are rarely pleasing in the long term. This is not to say that getting yourself a little pick-me-up is entirely wrong – just be cautious how you use this as a self-reward system. You do not want to reward yourself today, only to regret doing so tomorrow. When considering rewards, focus on those that are not "hollow" in nature.

You should also keep in mind that success builds success. Success in one area will propel you to further successful ventures.

> *Keep in mind that success builds success.*

So, by acknowledging your success, you acknowledge that you will be successful in the future as well.

How big does the accomplishment need to be? That's up to you. Even small accomplishments deserve your acknowledgement. Keep looking for ways to celebrate life.

EVERY day of our lives we are on the *verge* of making those slight **changes** that would make all the **difference**.

~Mignon McLaughlin

Every day is an **opportunity** to make a NEW happy ending.

~Author Unknown

Relationships Change

Consider yourself and those you love as works in progress, because they will never stay the same. Relationships grow and change. It is natural for them to evolve, and if they don't then something is amiss.

Recognize that changes in a relationship are not bad things. To try and keep a relationship with a specific "mold" or "box," is detrimental to the life of the relationship. Let your relationships grow and flourish.

Friends

My Grandfather used to say that if you have one true friend then you are very fortunate. If you have a few truly close friends who are REAL friends, the kind that will be there in good times or bad, it is better than having several people that you call "friends," but who are really just "associates."

True friends are those that know you for who you truly are, and still like you anyway. True friends are those that you can rely on and who are there for you, even when you don't ask them to be. There is a really interesting quote that my friend has hanging in his house that says:

> "A true friend isn't the one who you call to come and get you out of jail. A true friend is sitting beside you in the jail cell saying, 'Wow.... was that a wild trip, or what?'"

Patience

Be patient with yourself. You cannot change overnight. If there is something about yourself that you want to change, acknowledge that it will take time.

"Rome wasn't built in a day," nor can you snap your fingers and change something about yourself, be it your weight, a bad habit, learning a new skill...anything. If you are trying to change and you find yourself slipping back into your old habits, congratulate yourself for noticing, and put yourself back on the path you chose for yourself.

In addition to being patient with yourself, be patient with others who are trying to change and work on themselves as well. Encourage them. Acknowledge their struggle and celebrate their triumphs.

Acknowledge Your Uniqueness

You are unique. In the entire world, you are the only you that there is. Isn't it amazing?!?! Think of all the combinations of individuals who came together, across all of time, to form your parents.

Think of all the choices that were made by your parents from the beginning of their lives that eventually led to their union, which ultimately produced you!

Think about the fact that when you were conceived, that about 20,000 other sperm were fighting to unite with your mother's ovum, aside from the one that contained the unique genetic sequence that ultimately produced you! If one other sperm had united with the ovum, you would not have been. A few seconds or even *nanoseconds* would have made the difference.

Know that you are unique in all of space and time in this universe. Embrace the uniqueness of you.

Perfection Doesn't Exist

Accept that you are not perfect. Why would anyone want to be? Wouldn't it be boring if you did everything 100% correctly? You would have no thrill of accomplishment, no learning curve, no challenge to anything.

Even those who seem to have perfect lives on the outside are far from perfect. We look at those fabulous, "perfect" people on television…you know the ones…they have tons of money, beautiful homes, all the good looks…and inevitably we hear of some aspect of their life that is far from perfect. Whether they suffer from addictions, eating disorders,

> *Even those who seem to have perfect lives on the outside are far from perfect.*

relationship issues, etc., they have their share of problems and imperfections.

It is true that we all have our burdens, despite our place in life. People often say, "If I had a million dollars, I would have these problems," whatever those problems might be. This is a true statement. You would have a million dollars, and a whole new set of problems.

Be happy that you are not perfect. It would be more of a curse than a blessing.

Find Yourself A Good Doctor

It is essential that you find yourself a doctor you can trust, and one that is easy to talk to. Don't think that just any doctor will do. You need to find a medical provider with which you feel comfortable.

Make sure you tell your doctor everything. They are not mind readers, nor do they have any special powers that will let them deduce all your ailments, aches, or pains. You need to be completely open and honest with them. Keeping things from them serves no purpose.

Also, don't try to sugar coat things. If you don't exercise, just tell them. If you don't eat right, they need to know. If you drink or use illicit drugs, it is important for them to have this information. In order for them to help you, you need to give them a clear picture. If you want their help, tell them what they need to know.

Today you are YOU, THAT *is* truer THAN *true*. There is

no **one alive** *who* IS YOUER **than You.**

~ Dr. Seuss

The most IMPORTANT **thing** IN life *is* **TO** learn how *to* give *out* **love,** *and* **to** LET IT *come* **in.**

~Morrie Schwartz

It *is* **always** BETTER TO be *an* *original* THAN **an** *imitation.*

~Theodore Roosevelt

Look At The World Through The Eyes Of A Child

Look at the world around you with a sense of discovery. When we were children we explored with a sense of abandon, examining the most mundane aspects of our environment with excitement. As our lives become more involved, we forget to look at the world with a wide-eyed sense of wonder.

Take time to do that again. Look at things you have looked at many times before as if you are looking at them for the first time. You might be surprised what you see! Now....look at the people who mean the most to you with that same sense of wonderment, as if you are meeting them for the first time. Remember why they mean so much to you. Notice the feelings that move through you as you do this.

Appreciate every little aspect of life. Focus on these moments when things go awry. Enjoy the little things.

Self-Actualization

Lots of different psychological theorists talk about becoming "self-actualized." What exactly does this mean? Self-actualization, though defined differently by various theorists, means (according to Abraham Maslow) that an individual:

1. embraces facts and the truth, instead of denying them

2. is spontaneous

3. is interested in solving problems

4. accept themselves and others and lacks prejudice

While not everyone is self-actualized, and it is difficult to achieve, self-actualization is very good goal for which to strive. Do you always remain self-actualized once you get to that state? It depends on which expert you talk to as to the answer you will receive. Either way, strive for the goal, as it is a worthy pursuit.

Your Emotional Tool Box

Develop a "tool box" full of stress fighting techniques that you find work for you. Everything from breathing techniques, meditation, exercise, writing, and so on, can help to keep your stress manageable. The key is to know how to use these tools BEFORE you need them.

Learn what works and practice the technique before you need it. Take a little time each week to practice with your "tools." The more you use them, the more effective they will be.

Do What You Love

What types of activities bring you satisfaction? Gardening? Fishing? Spending time with your family? Take inventory of those things that bring you pleasure, satisfaction and fulfillment.

Once you have given this some thought, make a concentrated effort to do these things more often. It isn't selfish to take time to do things you enjoy, because it allows you to become more centered, and you will find that you are a more pleasant person, and people will want to be around you more! Enjoy life!

Give Someone A Call

When is the last time you called up your brother, sister, or a friend, just to see how they are doing? It is so easy to get caught up in the "noise" of life that we forget to pay attention to those who are the most important to our lives.

Make time for those who are important. Show them you care.

Go Off The Beaten Path

A GPS is a wonderful tool. "What," you say!?!?! "I input my destination and it takes me through obscure neighborhoods, back country roads, and I get frustrated!" My response is, "EXACTLY!"

A GPS will get you where you want to go, but it will take you via routes you would probably not have used if you were plotting the way yourself. Enjoy these little detours!

I have seen some exceptional architecture, found some interesting shops, and traveled through some beautiful countrysides all because I used my GPS. It gets me where I need or want to go....eventually. Don't have a GPS? So what? Drive! Walk! Explore! Don't be afraid to deviate from the "standard" path. Enjoy the journey! You can see some really interesting things along the way.

Routine Or Rut?

Routines. We all have them, and in many cases we are quite predictable. Try doing things differently one day.

As an example, most people, when they shave, do it exactly the same each time. Try starting on the opposite side once and a while, just to change things up a bit. Do you always eat the same type of things? Try something new. Do you always take the same route to or from work? Try a different route. As an example from my own life, I mowed the lawn the same way, with the same routine for over 20 years. Then, for whatever reason, I decided that one day I would mow it the opposite of the way I normally did. Guess what I discovered? Because I wasn't using the same old routine, I was actually able to mow it using 25% less gas, and it shaved approximately 30 minutes off of my work time! Now, I mow the lawn this "new" way, saving money and time.

Break your routines every once and a while and see what you might be missing by doing something differently. Go ahead. Try something new.

Smile!

While the truth about the "it takes more muscles to frown than to smile" aphorism is still undetermined, what science does know is that the human brain is "wired" to respond like-for-like, and that smiling, like yawning, is contagious.

Smile at everyone you meet and see what happens. The majority of them will smile back at you! Numerous researchers have indicated that this seems to hold true, with but a few exceptions. The other finding is that the simple act of smiling, even when you do not feel like doing such, lightens your mood. While it is not a "cure-all" it certainly won't hurt anything if you do it! Give it a try. Smile at everyone you meet. Smile when you feel down and glum. Notice how this one simple act can change your life in a positive way. You might be surprised at what you find!

Stay True To Your Values

Don't compromise your values. If following your passion means that you have to compromise your integrity or your values, walk away from that situation. It might take a while, but find another situation wherein you can do what you love in a way that is in sync with what you value.

Compromising what you believe can fill you with a sense of regret, which detracts from your sense of fulfillment. Sometimes doing what you believe to be right isn't easy, but know that it is the right thing to do, and you will sleep better at night in the security of knowing that you were true to yourself and that which you believe.

Let Your "Inner Child" Free

Feel like dancing? Go for it! Embrace your "inner child" and allow yourself to have fun. Think about how children dance and twirl, without regard for what "other people" will think.

What will people think if you were to do something silly like this? Who cares! If you feel like moving your feet...even if there is no music...do it! Generally, not only will you feel good, but it will bring a smile to most other people's faces as well. Some people might look at you like you are weird, but who cares? It is those people for whom we can feel sorry, because they don't know how to have fun.

By in large, people have forgotten how to have fun, and how to enjoy life as they did in their youth. Learn to liberate your inner freedom again. How? Simply do it. There is no "big secret." Have fun. Enjoy life. Dance!

Great is **the** MAN who

HAS *not lost* HIS CHILDLIKE

heart.

~Mencius

You can be CHILDLIKE

WITHOUT BEING

CHILDISH.

~Christopher Meloni

IN *every* REAL *man* **a child**

is HiddeN THAT WANTS

TO play.

~Fredrich Niezsche

What Do You Want To Be When You Grow Up?

When you were little, what did you want to do when you became an adult? What kind of response did you get from your elders? There are very few people who actually end up doing what they wanted to do as a child? Why?

Many times individuals are discouraged by the negative feedback they get from those around them. "You want to be an astronaut? Now don't be silly, you couldn't do that!" Look at it this way: Someone has to be an astronaut, why not you?

Indeed, some jobs have age restrictions, but if you are young enough, go for it! What if you (like me!) are older and cannot qualify based on your age? Is it possible to do something related that you may equally enjoy? Sure it is! Did you want to be a superhero? Obviously you can't do that. But the question we have to ask is, was it just the really cool super powers that attracted you, or was it the fact that superheroes help people in need? There are plenty of service related jobs out there, some with more "action" than others, wherein you can help people if that is what you want to do. Don't overlook your childhood dreams!

The Sky's The Limit

If you had unlimited time and money, what would you do? How would you spend it? Someone might respond to these questions with, "If I had the time and the money, I would open a restaurant." So how can you live this dream? At the present, you may not have the time or the money to open a restaurant, but you could cook some meals for friends. You could offer to make lunch for your co-workers.

The point is this: You can most likely approximate your goal, if you really want to do so. Ask yourself, "How can I make this happen?" Ask other people. Get ideas. Live to enjoy life, and do what you love!

Money Isn't Everything

Be cautious about doing things you truly love to do for money. Some people find that if they really enjoy doing something such as cooking, painting portraits, drawing, woodworking, crafting – anything really, and they try to make a business out of it, that it quickly loses its luster. Eventually they may end up not caring for it anymore at all.

Be cautious about doing things you truly love to do for money.

Your desire to do something is either based on an internal motivation or an external motivation. We are not as passionate about those things which we are externally motivated to do. When we do something we are passionate about, we do it because our passion is our motivation, which is internal. When money becomes the motivation, it is possible to lose interest.

On the other hand, when people do what they love, some people say, "I can't believe I get paid to do what I love!" You need to figure out which type of person you are before you decide to take something you love and turn it into a business.

The Right Time Is NOW

Don't wait for the perfect moment to do something. Do it NOW! Remember, nothing is perfect. If you are trying to wait until you get "this" or "that" accomplished before you do what you love, then you will be waiting forever. Something will always tarnish that perfect moment and you will fabricate another condition that has to be met before you do what you love.

Perfect moments are generally recognized after they have passed. Don't wait! Seize the moment!

The Importance Of Your Own Wants

Doing what you want to do isn't always selfish. Some people put their own wants second to everyone else's all the time. They feel what they want is unimportant. This isn't healthy.

A healthy relationship, be it a marriage, a friendship, or a parent/child relationship, involve compromise, giving and taking, and balance. You are entitled to having your wants fulfilled occasionally, as is everyone else, as long as it is within reason.

What's the worst possible thing that can happen, if you do what you want to do? I'm not referring to anything immoral or illegal. I'm talking about things like eating a restaurant where you would like to eat, going somewhere you would like to go, or something akin to this. Will the world end? No. Will life as we know it cease? No.

Go ahead. Acknowledge that your wants are important. Know that your opinions and thoughts matter.

Emotions Are Normal

Understand that it is OK to feel anger, depression, and anxiety...all those emotions which have negative connotations. One of the greatest misconceptions that people have is that if they have to take medication for depression or anxiety is that they will cease to be anxious or depressed. Not the case. These emotions are normal and healthy. Medication only brings them within a manageable range and doesn't eliminate them. You will still feel depressed or anxious, but not *as* depressed or anxious.

Don't feel that if you experience these emotions, even if you are NOT on medication, that something is wrong. Quite the contrary, everything is right. It is when these emotions become overwhelming that they become problematic.

Embrace your emotions, secure in the knowledge that they belong to you, and you are entitled to feel them. Don't beat yourself up for being human!

ONE'S **suffering** DISAPPEARS

When *one* LETS ONESELF **go**, *when*

one yields – *even* to
sadness.
~Antoine de Saint-Exupéry

A *man* WHO *is* MASTER OF himself

CAN **end a sorrow** *as* easily AS HE **can**

invent A PLEASURE.
~Oscar Wilde

Anger

Everyone gets angry. But how do you deal with it to keep your anger under control?

1. First you need to learn to recognize when you are getting angry. Notice if you feel your muscles begin to tense (or your fists), you feel a flush, you frown and scowl: Learn to become aware of when this happens. It will help you to maintain control.

2. Next, accept your anger. Reacting to a situation is fine, but over-reacting doesn't help anyone. Know that it is OK to get angry, but that it is not OK to fly off the handle. Acknowledge that you are getting angry.

3. Relax. Relaxing is something that you need to practice doing before you need it. Refer to Page 19 on tips for relaxation. Utilize these at this stage.

4. Think about ways to express your anger. Don't try to edit or filter your thoughts. Let them flow. Think about various different ways to express your feelings.

5. Evaluate the consequences of a thought as it enters your mind. Ask yourself what will happen to you or the other person if you act on this particular thought. Will you hurt someone's feelings? Will you regret it later? Will you go to jail....? Ask yourself if this is an appropriate reaction or if it is an over-reaction?

6. Choose the best alternative. Which of the reactions is the best course of action?

7. Express your anger. It is not healthy to keep things bottled up inside of you. In some way, your anger will manifest. After choosing the **best** way to express yourself, do it.

Dream The Impossible Dream

What are the barriers to you pursuing your goals or dreams? What is keeping you from taking that first step toward realizing your dreams? Critically examine these road blocks. What can you realistically do to begin eliminating them? Don't simply assume you cannot do something, and that is your "reason" for not doing it.

Break the process of accomplishing your dreams down in to small do-able tasks. As an example, if you dream of having a job in another country, you can do a simple internet search to see what kinds of jobs are available in those countries. Work from that point to see what you may be qualified to do. Apply for those jobs. Sooner or later, you will be able to realize your dream. Things are often not as difficult as we make them out to be!

Failures

You attempt something and you are not successful. This could be anything from a lifestyle change to starting a business. Have you failed?

It depends on how you define failure. You can look at your failure as either a stumbling block, or as a wall. A stumbling block is just something that temporarily sets you back. A wall prevents you from continuing.

Learn from your experiences. As long as you learn something from the experience, even if it is how NOT to do whatever it was that you were attempting, it is NOT A FAILURE. It is a learning experience, and that is a success. Thomas Edison made over 10,000 attempts to make the first commercially practical incandescent light. (He didn't actually invent the light bulb, as many people think. It was invented in 1809 by Humphrey Davy.) When asked about all his failures, he simply said, "I have not failed. I've just found 10,000 ways that won't work."

Remember, how you think about life and your experiences is responsible for how you feel about them.

Learn From The Negative

We all have negative experiences in our life. We all have those situations which we would rather not have occurred. The important thing to remember is that as long as we LEARN from those experiences, they are not entirely bad.

> *Learn from your mistakes.*

Take the lessons you learn from these experiences with you and apply them to you in the NOW.

Learn from the things happen that you cannot control. When something bad happens or you make a mistake, ask yourself, "What can this teach me?" As long as you are learning, you are growing. Don't dwell on these issues and allow them to bring you down.

THERE ARE NO failures –
JUST *experiences* and **your**
reactions TO **them**.

~Tom Krause

Courage DOESN'T *always* ROAR.
Sometimes **COURAGE** IS that
QUIET VOICE AT tHe END **of the** DAY
SAYING, "**I will** TRY again *tomorrow*.

~Mary Anne Radmacher

Many of LIFE'S FaiLureS ARE MEN WHo
DID NOT *realize* **how** CLOSE **they** were
to SUCCESS when **they** GAVE up.

~Thomas Edison

You Are Never Too Old!

People say, "I'm too old to learn that," or, "I wish I would have done this when I was younger." The truth is that it is never too late to follow your dreams.

I have heard people say, "I would like to go to college, but I'm too old now..." These are people in their late 30's or 40's. Immediately I relay to

> *It is never too late to follow your dreams.*

them that I have had a number of students in college who didn't start until they were in their 70's. I even had one student in her 80's, and she graduated!

Don't let age be your excuse. Find something new to try. If you have ever wanted to try something new, do it! You'll be surprised at what you can accomplish!

Success Is Yours

Success is what you as an individual define it to be. Don't let other people define what it means for you to be successful. If you let other people define what makes you successful, then you are allowing them to set your standards.

Set your own standards based on your individual happiness. Some people who appear to be highly successful are also highly miserable. Some people who appear to be unsuccessful, at least according to society, are very happy. Who then is truly the success?

What does success mean to you? Having a place to live? Being able to pay your bills? Having enough to eat? Having friends....true friends?

Focus on what success means to you and define it by your own standards. Celebrate your successes!

Laughter....The Best Medicine

Humor is one of the best ways to deal with stress and frustrations in your life. Spend time with family and friends who make you laugh. Watch a comedy TV show or movie.

Make it your personal goal to genuinely laugh.

Many times we laugh with others, but we are really only laughing to be sociable. That's fine, but consciously put yourself with people and in situations that you know you will enjoy. You can fake laughing until you make it, but putting yourself in situations where the laughter could be real increases your odds of enjoying yourself. Laugh! Enjoy life!

Stress

There are two types of stress: Positive stress, known as "eustress", and negative stress which is called, "distress." Most of the time when we refer to stress, we are talking about the bad kind, and it can be rather taxing.

Stress is impossible to eliminate. Understand that. Sometimes it is possible to eliminate that "thing" or situation that is contributing to our stress, and sometimes it is not.

With practice it is possible to minimize the effects that stress can have on our daily lives.

What you can do is learn to control your reaction to stress. Learn to know what things you can change and change them, and acknowledge those things that are beyond your ability to change. Through acceptance and understanding you can reduce the stress that you encounter.

Personal Warning Signals

It is essential that you try to recognize emotional and physical "red flags" that act as warning signs that stress is beginning to take hold of you. Muscle aches and pains, diarrhea or constipation, craving for "comfort foods," skin problems, forgetfulness, sleeping more or sleeping less – are all signs that you need to slow down and relax.

If you notice that you are getting a cold, slow down. Sometimes getting sick is your bodies way of saying, "You are running on empty...you need to slow down!"

Make sure you consult with your physician about any sudden changes in your "system," as they could be warning signs of more serious problems. Don't let something get out of hand.

Take time to recharge your batteries. Being aware of your personal "red flags" can help you in a multitude of ways. Know them, and be well.

LIFE *is* NOT MERELY **to** BE alive,

BUT to be *well*.

~Marcus Valerius Martial

I AM PRETTY *sure* that, if **you WILL** be
quite *honest,* **you** will ADMIT THAT **a
good** rousing **sneeze,** ONE THAT tears
OPEN *your* COLLAR **and** tHROWS your
HAIR **into** YOUR eyes, **is** REALLY
one OF **life's** SENSATIONAL
PLEASURES.

~Robert Benchley

I believe THAT we cannot **LIVE**

better *than* IN *seeking* TO
BECOME **BETTER**.

~Socrates

Social Interest

"Social interest" or in German, "gemeinshaftsgefühl" is a term coined by Alfred Adler and refers to one's "sense of community" or contribution to the common good or welfare. Adler postulated that the healthy individual is one who has a strong social interest. What this means is that, when you contribute to the betterment of society, you are generally more emotionally healthy.

One of the things I encourage clients to do is to become active. Contributing to society, in even small ways, not only increases your activity, but it in turn gives you a sense of satisfaction, knowing that you have done something that will possibly make the world a better place.

How can you contribute? It could be in any number of ways. Help with food drives, volunteer at a nursing home or library...the options are only limited by your imagination.

To Sleep, Perchance To Dream

Make sure you get enough sleep. Various studies have shown that sleep deprivation increases stress related hormones. An excess of these hormones in your system can increase your risk of hypertension, stroke, heart attack, or other cardiovascular problems. Not getting enough sleep can also contribute to a lowering of your immune system's defenses.

Make sure you get enough sleep every night. Some people need more sleep than others. Listen to your body. Sleep. Rest. Dream.

You Can Teach An Old Dog New Tricks

Living in the NOW involves always taking time to learn something that you previously did not know. You are never too old to learn something new.

After 40 years, I'm happy to report that I learned how to swim! Am I a good swimmer? No. But, I'm learning more each day. You can do the same. Obviously it doesn't have to be swimming, but you can learn a new skill no matter your age.

It is true that it may take you a bit longer to learn something new later in life than you could have earlier in your life. Equally true is the fact that you may not be able to do it like you could have when you were younger. But still...embrace the idea that there is an entire world of new things to learn, and that you can find something.

If, by learning something new you are trying to do it to "prove yourself," then you need to evaluate if you are doing it for the right reasons. If you are learning something simply for the enjoyment of doing, then you are on the right track. Challenge yourself to learn something new. It can be rewarding on many different levels.

Create Your Life

Life is so very serious at times. Still, this does not mean that you have to be serious all the time. Look for the humor in life. Take time to enjoy your family, your friends, and what you have around you. Doing this will enrich your life.

Put yourself into situations you can enjoy. Far too many times we find ourselves thrust into situations which are stressful, and far from enjoyable. Make a conscious effort to create enjoyable situations. Doing so allows you to be more in control of your moods and your personal satisfaction, rather than allowing it to be at the whim of the environment.

An Appointment With Fun

The adage, "All work and no play makes Jack a dull boy," is very true. Not taking time to enjoy yourself can lead to a very unexciting and unfulfilled life.

Schedule a time for enjoyment and fun, and keep the "appointment" with yourself as you would a doctor's appointment or some other appointment that you are reluctant to skip. There have been times when I have given my clients appointments with

Make an "appointment" with family or friends, and then schedule other things around it.

themselves and asked them to be sure they keep them. I've even gone so far as to make them out an appointment card to remember the time and commitment.

If you keep waiting for the right time to go on vacation or to go out to dinner or to simply spend time alone or go on a picnic, then it will not happen. Schedule it, do it, and enjoy it.

Lend A Helping Hand

Helping others is a way of helping yourself. Remember, your "cup" must be full in order to give someone else a drink, so you need to take care of yourself, and take time to fill your "cup." But when you can, and when it doesn't have a negative effect on you, help others. How can you do this? Here are some ideas:

- Smile at others

- Be friendly and talk with others

- Volunteer – not for everything, but for one or two causes you feel are worthwhile

- Donate something you no longer use

- Teach others when you can

- Donate food

- Be patient when others are struggling

- Publicly show your appreciation for someone

- Create a care package for the sick, elderly, homeless, or for someone in the military

- Recycle

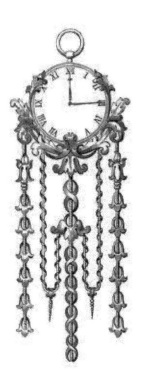

How far THAT little **candle** throws *his* beams! **So** shines *a* **good deed** IN A **weary WORLD**.

~ *William Shakespeare*

WE ARE **always** GETTING READY to **live but** NEVER **living.**

~ Ralph Waldo Emerson

Family Time

Family is very important, and having fun with your family is essential to the life and health of your relationships. What are some things that you can do with your family to have fun and not spend a fortune doing so? Try these on for size:

- Read books together. Talk about the plot and the characters. If you have young children, read to them. As they get older, read with them.

- Watch TV together. Sometimes the television needs turned off to spend quality time together. However, in moderation you can find some interesting shows that everyone likes and you can watch them together.

- Go camping. You need not travel to the mountains to do this...try camping in your back yard or at a local park.

- Go to the beach...if you are fortunate enough to live close to one. My family has to drive for a number of hours to get to the nearest beach, but if you live close enough, take advantage of it.

- Play a board game, dominoes, charades, etc. Some games can be fun and educational. We are teaching my son to count money and give back change by playing Monopoly.

- Cook something together. There is something (at least for me) relaxing about chopping and slicing ingredients for a meal. Children love to mix and stir, and as they get older, they like to chop and slice. Instead of looking at a meal as a chore, look at it as an opportunity for togetherness, and use it as a time to talk and share with each other.

- Go to a museum. Look at the exhibits, be they art, history, or whatever. Talk about them and how weird or odd they are. Enjoy just being together and seeing things to which you may not have been exposed.

- Visit the library. Many libraries have programs for children and adults. Also, libraries have computer access, so if you can't afford high speed internet at home, your library might be able to accommodate your internet needs.

Family Meal Time

During meal time ask everyone about their day. Keeping communication open is essential to a healthy family dynamic. Make sure that everyone has the opportunity to talk. Have family members tell about the events they find important. Laugh and joke during meal time.

One word of caution to parents: Stay away from conversations about being in trouble at school, or similarly disturbing topics. Mealtime should be a time when people come together in unity, and should not be a time of discomfort.

What are some conversation starters for mealtime conversation? Try these on for size:

- Name 3 things you have never done but would like to do.

- If you were ruler for a day, how would things change?

- What is your favorite place in the world? Why?

- How do you think you belly button got it's name?

- What would you like to invent?

Keep looking for new ways to bring conversation to the table. Your life will be better for it!

Enjoy Nature

Play outside together! It doesn't make any difference if you are 6 or 60, you can still enjoy a walk in a summer rain, a roll in the leaves during the fall, the brisk pureness of a winter snow, or the brilliant flowers of spring. Enjoy what all the seasons have to offer.

Go for a hike. Explore nature, or if you live in the city, take a stroll down different streets and see what your city has to offer. Life is an adventure if you let it be! Live it!

The Unexamined Life

Socrates is credited as having said, "The unexamined life is not worth living." Given this, if you are reading this book then indeed you are examining your life, and thus trying to be more than you were in the proverbial yesterday. To guide you in your quest for self-examination ask yourself the following questions:

- Who is important to me? Who do I love? What am I doing to show them I love them and that they are important to me?

- Am I following my dream(s)? What keeps me from doing this?

- Am I contributing to the well-being of others?

- Have I made someone smile today?

- What can I do to be more than I was yesterday?

To Everything Its Season

Keep in mind that everything has a time and a place. If a technique you have tried and used successfully in the past isn't working in the NOW, don't fret...just try something new. An example of this might be, trying to get your family to communicate. Know that you can't force communication. All you can do is provide opportunities that facilitate communication. Trying to force an idea or to attempt to "make" them have fun or communicate will be counter-productive and will most likely frustrate you. Another example might be trying to lose weight. Perhaps you have hit a plateau, and the techniques you have used in the past aren't working. If this happens, try a new technique that will get you over the "hump." Something will eventually work.

Don't give up on things that are within your power, but remember to acknowledge that you can only change yourself. You have to accept that things change, and that in spite of your best attempts to alter circumstances you may not be successful. Change what you can, and accept what you cannot. If, you have tried and tried to "pull things together" and cannot, perhaps you need to look toward accepting that the time and place to accomplish this has past.

Reframing

Sometimes in therapy we try to help people "reframe" their problems. Reframing is a process whereby you have been looking at an issue one way, and one way only. In reframing, we try to get you to look at it from a different perspective.

For instance, let's say that you have a teenager who feels that their mother is overly protective of them, not letting them do anything or go anywhere by themselves. Reframing would involve a process whereby you help the person to understand that instead of being over-protective, the mother just loves them so much they want to make sure that they are safe because they are the most precious thing in their mother's life. In other words, the mother isn't doing this to be mean, but is instead, in her own way, demonstrating her love and concern for her child. Daily life is chocked full of situations that, if we think about them, we can see that the motives we ascribe to other people for their actions isn't at all what we are making them out to be.

Another example of reframing is taking the "lemons" of life and making "lemonade." The story of the famous singer Julio Igleasias is an example. He was once a promising soccer player, but an accident left him semi-paralyzed. While he was in the hospital, a nurse brought him a guitar, and he began to practice playing and singing. Eventually Julio went on to hold a Guinness Book of World Record for the "most albums sold in all languages."

Using the technique of reframing allows us to see the world from a completely different perspective. Try it sometime, and see how it works for you. You may be pleasantly surprised!

Negativity

My Karate instructor taught us that CAN'T is a FOUR LETTER WORD. It seems like so many are taught, mostly through observation and imitation, to be negative, or that they can't do something.

Trying to be positive doesn't happen overnight. It

> *"Can't,"*
> *never did and never will.*

can take a while, and it does take practice. Think about this, "When the storm hits and the rain comes--- learn to dance in the rain!!!" Negativity is contagious. Learn to avoid it. How? Previously, we talked about reframing. This is one possible way to attempt to counter negativity. Think about ways to reframe the negative into the positive.

The BAD "What If?"

People get caught up in thinking about "What If?" Instead of using this as a creative process, (which is discussed next) they dwell on negative "What If's?" Dwelling on negative possibilities can literally cause you to work yourself into a panic.

People will often say, "What if....," and then they fill in some possible catastrophic life event, " happens, then I'll....," and they fill in some equally catastrophic potential consequence. When clients do this, I will often ask them, "What if a meteor comes crashing through the roof right now, and wipes us out? Should I begin living my life as if it will? Should I build a bunker to live in, and never go outside? Or, would it be better for me to be outside where I could see it coming? What should I do?" They will often look at me as if to say, "Well.....that's just silly." When you think about it, the idea that we should continually worry about bad things happening in our lives, whatever they might be, is the same. This illustration begins to point out what a waste of energy it is to worry all the time.

The point is we cannot worry about "What If?" Nor can we live our lives by "What If?" We need to focus on what IS, and not "What If?" By focusing on what IS, you live in the NOW. By focusing on "What If?" you are putting your energy into some future event, over which you have no control, and in the process take away from the NOW. Remember, focus on what IS, not the terrible "What If?"

The GOOD "What If?"

Having talked about the BAD "What If?" let's talk about the GOOD "What If?" Instead of using "What If?" to focus on negative possibilities, use it to focus on good ones! Use it to spark creativity!

Use the GOOD "What If?" to shape your NOW, so that in the future your goals and dreams can be realized! As an example: What if you didn't have to worry about money? How would your life be different? What types of things would you do? Now....the question becomes, how can you make that happen? What if you could make just a few changes that would allow these dreams to come true, if only partially? Don't like that example?

Try this one. Imagine you are back in time (really....humor me here...) about 20 years or so. Imagine you are the person who said, "What if students didn't have to go to class and could still get credit? What if we used the internet to deliver coursework to them, and they could get a degree online?" Now, come back to the present. Look at all the online universities that exist.

Now, think about the power of possibility. Ask yourself...."What if?" and let your creativity flow.

Memory Woes

"Wouldn't you like to be able to remember more, and be able to recall things more accurately? How would you like to develop a better than photographic memory? Well you can, and it isn't as difficult as you might believe."

Does this sound like an infomercial? Indeed it does. However, I can legitimately say that there is one authoritative source for memory improvement that has NEVER failed me, and the claims are absolutely TRUE.

Harry Lorayne's memory systems are by far the most simple, yet most effective methods of improving your memory. We could spend page after page detailing various memory techniques, but why? Everything you need to know can be learned from his material. Do you want to learn how to memorize a list of 20-30 or more objects, and then repeat them both forward and backward? Use the LINK technique, which you can learn in about 2 minutes. Imagine, in 2 minutes being able to do something that you probably never thought possible before. Check out his website at:

www.harrylorayne.com

We ALL have *our* time MACHINES.
Some take US BACK, they're *called*
memories. *Some take* us forward,
they're CALLED DREAMS.

~Jeremy Irons

THE HEART *that* truly *loves*
never forgets.

~Jewish Proverb

MEMORY IS THE diary that
we *all* CARRY about WITH us.

~Oscar Wilde

Families

I once had a professor tell me that approximately 80% of families in the United States are chronically dysfunctional. While I cannot find any sources to support his assertion, my personal experience in dealing with clients and their families suggests that this is not out of the realm of possibility.

Understand that ALL families have their "weirdnesses." What is "normal" to you and your family may seem completely alien to another family. Families are strange beasts on the best of days. It seems that the one place people should feel safe and secure is many times the place that causes them the most distress.

So how do you deal with it? Change what you can....yourself. A family is a system, and a powerful one at that. You may need to make some profound changes in your life, and perhaps even cut ties, in order to be healthy.

Know that you are the only part of the system over which you have control. Love your family, but know your limitations. If the dysfunction pulls you in and "sucks the life" from you, know that you have the power to change.

Life's Complications

When life gets complicated, is it because the world is complicated or because we are complicated? Is life complicated? Sure, sometimes. But people have this wonderful gift for making things more complex than they need to be.

Why do we make things complicated? The reasons are as many and varied as you can count. When you feel like things are getting complicated, take a step back and examine how you can possibly simplify them. Utilize the old KISS method i.e., "Keep It Simple, Silly!" What does this mean? It means that you should simplify things whenever possible.

Question yourself about everything. Ask, "Why do I do this?" "Why is this important?" "What would happen if I didn't do this?" Focus on streamlining. Perhaps you cannot simplify. Then again, until you try, you will never know!

Take Time to Smell the Roses

Slow down, relax. Living in the NOW involves appreciating the moment. Have you ever literally stopped to smell the roses?

Try it some time! Take time to look at things, touch them, smell them, and taste them...whatever! When you go to the grocery store, smell the produce. When you pass a vendor giving samples of food items, give them a taste. When you see a flower, stop and smell it. When you see something with an interesting texture, take time to feel it.

Slowing down in little ways has a cumulative effect. Lots of little moments can add up to a more focused life in the NOW. Enjoy your moments.

Compete with Yourself

While contests to see who is the fastest or best have their place, the best person to be in a contest with is you. Try to better yourself or improve yourself. Don't worry about what everyone else is doing, or how well they can do something. Focus on where you are and what you are able to do.

As an example, my wife and I recently elected to lose some weight. While we elected to do it together, we were not in a competition with each other. We supported each other, and only focused on our individual results.

When my wife started, her weight loss consultant asked her she were losing weight because she wanted to do so, or was it for me. She replied, telling the individual that she was doing it for herself…to which they responded, "Good! Losing weight for someone else is the best way to fail."

By competing with yourself you will find that you can become more than what you are at the present. Challenge yourself. Do things because YOU want to do them. You might be surprised at what you can accomplish!

You Can't Make Me

I often chuckle when I hear people say things like, "They made me mad," or "They make me feel so inferior." Why do I find it amusing? Because other people cannot make you feel anything.

Feelings come from within, not from outside. Ask a person how someone "made" them mad, and they will say something like, "They did this…"or, "they did that…and it made me mad." The truth is, it isn't them that made you angry or feel inferior, or feel...whatever..., it is how you interpreted the act that makes you feel the way you do. You get angry...people don't make you angry. Other people do not have a magic remote control that allows them to control your feelings.

You and you alone are responsible for how you feel. Sure...you can get angry at someone, but don't fool yourself into thinking they made you feel that way.

"Vampires"

Are there "vampires" in your life? These are people who, when you are around them, just drain you of positivity, energy, etc. I know one person in particular that, almost without exception, people like...but they don't want to be around them for any length of time because the individual wears them out. Simply by being around them and talking to them, one begins to feel drained, emotionally speaking.

In general these "vampires" don't realize that they have this effect on other people. Still, just because the person doesn't know that you react to them in this manner doesn't detract from the effect on your life.

How do you handle these people? Simple! Try not to be around them any more than necessary. Next, be very self-aware of when you are starting to feel drained. Find a way to politely excuse yourself from the situation.

Can you always do this? No. Sometimes you may have to contend with the situation. If this happens, find a way to energize yourself as soon as possible following the encounter.

Who are the "vampires" in your life? What strategies can you use to avoid them?

Drama

There are people whose lives seem to be constantly enthralled in drama. How do you deal with these people? Stay focused on the NOW. Many times these people are caught up in situations and circumstances (often as a result of their own inability to resolve issues), and they attempt to pull you into their chaos. How do you deal with these people? Keep these things in mind:

- Don't get involved in their drama.

- Don't worry about it.

- Don't feed into it.

- Understand that the drama will pass.

Keep in mind that many times drama "infested" people are often trying to get a reaction out of you. If, when they present you with their production, you play it off as though it doesn't really bother you (even if perhaps it does), then they will have the proverbial wind taken from their sails. Continue this when they are engaged in dramatic behavior, and by consistently not feeding into their drama, eventually they will leave you alone. At this point they will usually find someone else who is interested in their plight.

Go with the Flow

Learning to "roll with the punches" is essential to living a fulfilled life. How do you do it?

First, learn to let go. Easier said than done, right? It may take time, but have faith in yourself that you can let go and not take things personally and not be so hard on yourself.

Next, figure out what you know to be the facts of the situation. Don't allow yourself to be pulled into an emotional state. Keep your mind focused on what you know. After you have determined the facts, focus on the reality and don't catastrophize.

Finally, decide what course of action is the best and what you should do. Changing what has transpired isn't an option. Recognize this as a fact and move on to handle things, making the most of the situation. Above all RELAX!

The Oak and the Reeds

A very large Oak was uprooted by the wind and thrown across a stream. It fell among some Reeds, which it thus addressed: "I wonder how you, who are so light and weak, are not entirely crushed by these strong winds."

They replied, "You fight and contend with the wind, and consequently you are destroyed; but we bow and yield to every breeze, and thus the gale passed harmlessly over our heads.

~ Aesop

You Matter!

Give yourself some credit! You are just as good as anyone else. Some people focus on their personal inadequacies and as a result feel they are not as good as others.

No matter who you are, there will always be someone better looking, faster, stronger, wealthier, etc. Keep in mind likewise, that no matter who you are, there is always someone who is not as good looking, slower, weaker, who has less money than you, etc.

You are as good as anyone else, and don't forget it! You are entitled to your opinions, in spite of what the "experts" say. You are entitled to your beliefs, no matter what they may be. Personally, I would encourage you to base your beliefs and opinions on facts, but which facts you choose to believe is your business. Do not discount yourself! Believe in you!

Enjoy Yourself

Take time to play and enjoy yourself. It doesn't make any difference how old you are, let your inner child go and play. Swing on a swing, slide down a slide, climb on the monkey bars...have fun! Do cartwheels (if you can...for me it is difficult, but I pull them off every once and a while!), play video games, enjoy a good game of Monopoly or Spades.

> *Take time to play and enjoy yourself.*

Do something that is mindlessly fun and keeps you young at heart. True, as we get older our bodies don't allow us to do the things we used to do as readily as we used to do them. But, that does not mean that you have to do nothing.

Enjoy your life, because this is the only one you'll get! Have fun!

Nurture Your Creativity

Find a way to express yourself creatively. You don't need to be a concert pianist to enjoy playing the piano. Nor do you need to be an excellent artist to enjoy drawing.

Find something that you can do that is a way to access your creative side. Draw. Paint. Grow a garden. Write a poem. Do needlepoint. Anything! As long as you enjoy doing it, go for it! Nurture the artist inside of you.

Personal Finance Issues

Financial concerns are an issue that causes many people quite a bit of stress. Sometimes the answer to resolving your financial woes isn't as easy as getting another job. Some people find themselves in a financial crisis that is a result of outside events. How do you cope?

The answer to this question is, "As best you can." Know that if you work toward resolving your issue, even a little each day, or a bit every week, then you are on your way to overcoming it at some point.

Conversely, there are some everyday things you can do in order to help your finances. For some suggestions, refer to page 139 in the appendix. As with other aspects of your life, focus on your successes in trying to resolve your financial issues. Understand that you are human, and that things happen. Don't beat yourself up for these setbacks, and certainly don't depreciate your value as a human because of them.

HALT!

There are times when people are more approachable than others, and likewise, there are times when you are more approachable than others. One rule of thumb is to remember the HALT acronym when dealing with others, or when making a decision.

Try to never talk to someone about a serious issue or a decision when they are **H**ungry, **A**ngry, **L**onely or **T**ired. Think about how you are when you are in any one of these states, let alone a combination of them. You might find yourself observing that, "When I'm hungry, I'm a grouch butt! When I'm tired, I'm snippy!"

By not engaging in serious conversation when either party is in HALT mode, you are more likely to communicate more successfully.

Difficult People

We all have those people in our lives that we find to be difficult. How do you deal with these people?

- Wait them out. They might not always be around to aggravate you.

- Don't respond to them with "knee jerk" reactions. Give yourself time to think about your responses to them.

- Remove yourself from them, i.e. go for a walk, get a breath of fresh air.

- Avoid heated discussions.

- Kill them with kindness.

Try to be as patient as possible. Keep in mind that to some people YOU are a difficult person to deal with as well!

APPENDIX

Low Cost/No Cost Ways to Celebrate

- Take a long hot bath

- Go for a long walk

- Read a book

- Visit a library

- Make a time capsule

- Go stargazing

- Watch an old movie

- Find something to do off of the community calendar

- Take some photos

- Have a potluck dinner party with some friends

- Make paper airplanes

- Take a nap

- Go swimming

- Play with your pet

- Play video games

- Go on a bike ride

- Enjoy a nice cup of coffee or tea

- Watch a marathon of your favorite TV shows

- Listen to your favorite music

- Go backyard camping with your family

- Have friends over for a game night

- Attend an art gallery event

- Attend an open mic night at a coffee shop

- Be creative! Do whatever brings you enjoyment!

20 Ways To Be Romantic

- Leave a note on his/her pillow

- Make a CD with music that is meaningful to your relationship

- Dedicate a song to your partner on the radio

- Mail a romantic card to their place of work

- Write a romantic poem and give it to your partner

- Send flowers, unexpectedly

- Serve your partner breakfast in bed

- Make your partner a GIANT romantic card out of a big cardboard box

- Write "I Love You" in soap on the bathroom mirror

- Have your partner's portrait painted from a photograph they like

- Brush their hair, or give a back rub

- Write them a note, and insert it in a book they are reading

- Watch the sunset together

- Go on a picnic

- Throw a "Just Because" party to celebrate your partner

- Give them a key inscribed, "The Key To My Heart."

- Cook your partner a romantic meal, and eat it by candlelight

- On your partner's birthday, send their mother a "Thank You" card

- Go for a walk and hold hands

- Attend a concert together

20 Ways To Save Money

- Go out to eat less

- Make your own coffee

- Buy generic products whenever possible

- Consolidate and pay off debt as soon as possible

- Adjust your thermostat

- Use low energy light bulbs

- Shut windows and doors

- Check your phone service to see if they can save you money

- Change washing machine settings to use less energy

- Use cruise control to get better gas mileage

- Use coupons

- Buy in bulk

- Shop for bargains

- Look for end of season bargains

- Use only one credit card, and then only when needed

- Have movie night at home instead of going to the cinema

- Find a bank that has free checking. Change banks to one who has no hidden fees.

- Go grocery shopping with a list, and stick to it

- See if you can bundle your internet, telephone, and cable bill

- Give up unhealthy habits, such as smoking

Made in the USA
San Bernardino, CA
20 April 2019